THE GREAT PHILOSOPHERS

Consulting Editors
Ray Monk and Frederic Raphael

POPPER

Raphael Frederic

ROUTLEDGE
New York

Published in 1999 by
Routledge
29 West 35th Street
New York, NY 10001

First published in 1997 by
Phoenix
A Division of the Orion Publishing Group Ltd.
Orion House
5 Upper Saint Martin's Lane
London WC2H 9EA

10 9 8 7 6 5 4 3 2 1

Library of Congress Cataloging-in-Publication Data

Raphael, Frederic, 1931–
        Popper / Frederic Raphael.
         p. cm.—(The great philosophers : 16)
        Includes bibliographical references.
        ISBN 0-415-92391-3 (pbk.)
        1. Popper, Karl Raimund, Sir, 1902– . I. Title. II.
        Series: Great Philosophers (Routledge (Firm)) : 16.
B1649.P64R36 1999
192—dc21   99-22646
                                                 CIP

KARL POPPER

Historicism and Its Poverty

LIFE AND WORKS

Karl Raimund Popper was born in Vienna on 28 July 1902. His parents were of Jewish origin, though they had converted to Protestantism. His father, Simon, was an intellectual and a lawyer whose library was said to contain 15,000 volumes. Portraits of Schopenhauer and Darwin hung in his study. Karl's mother, Jenny Schiff, had a passion for music, which Popper shared. He thought of devoting himself to music as a young man and, as an amateur composer, he remained dedicated to it all his life.

Popper began to grow up in the fertile decadence of the Austro-Hungarian empire. A precocious scholar, he enrolled in the University of Vienna in 1918, though he did not become a matriculated student until 1922, by which time Austria had been shrivelled, by the Treaty of Versailles, to a small republic. The consequent inflation reduced his family to something like poverty. As a university student, Popper survived through teaching (mathematics, physics and chemistry) and, for a while, as a cabinet-maker.

He also involved himself in the political activities which followed the dissolution of the empire. At first a socialist, he became a communist in 1919. After a few months, however, he was appalled by the wilful bloodshed during Béla Kun's brief régime in neighbouring Hungary and disgusted by the speciousness of Marxist arguments justifying revolutionary violence. The prospect of an Ideal State, somewhere over the capitalist horizon, could not reconcile him to a programme of human sacrifice. If he continued to consider himself a socialist, he meant nothing more doctrinaire than that he believed in social justice. Eventually, in line with the views of Friedrich von Hayek, to whose thought he displayed an unusual measure of deference, he came to regard state socialism as a form of oppression. Freedom, he then argued, mattered more than equality; if freedom were lost or abandoned, equality itself could not be maintained among those who were not free.

The collapse of the Austro-Hungarian empire did not prevent Vienna from remaining a centre of intellectual vigour. The desire for a commanding post-imperial philosophy of life was fostered by political disintegration. Freud, Adler, Einstein and the so-called Vienna Circle of positivist philosophers, led by Moritz Schlick (who was later gunned down by a crazed student), propounded hypotheses of more or less durable worth, in all of which Popper became more or less durably interested. Elsewhere, Marxism was constantly advanced as the answer to political confusion and economic turmoil. So too, quite soon, was National Socialism.

Einstein stimulated Popper's enthusiasm for physics. What distinguished Einstein from Marx, Freud and Adler was that his ideas were susceptible of test, and hence of refutation. For instance, before Einstein's Theory of Relativity could be said to be valid, a particular event had had to take place, in the Solar System, which was impossible according to classic Newtonian principles. When a star's rays were indeed seen to be bent, by the gravitational pull of the sun, Einstein's prediction was fulfilled. Relativity had survived a key test that might have led to its refutation. This single instance had not proved Einstein to be entirely right, only right*er* than the now refuted Newton. Since there were only two eligible competitors, Einstein's theory was temporarily triumphant, but not *unquestionably* or conclusively.

Popper never cared to doubt the reality or the existence of the physical world. In order for physics and science to supply reliable foundations for civilization, he maintained that we have to accept that what is 'out there' is, however complicated or improbable, real. Thus many of the obsessions of English empirical philosophy remained alien to him: neither phenomenalism nor the problem of knowledge detained him for long. What *we* know, he was disposed to think, is more important than whether or how *I* know. *Cogitamus* was more important than any *cogito*.

Popper came early to the keystone of his idea of scientific method: scientists proved their good faith by seeking the most stringent possible ways of *falsifying* their hypothesis – that is, of detecting flaws in their own work. Any idea that cannot conceivably be refuted is not scientific. It may, however, have interest-value for other reasons. In the light of this cautious generosity, Popper could argue – against the philosophical current both in Vienna and, later, in England – that metaphysics was *not* a useless subject. What he did challenge, implacably, was 'scientism', which involved metaphysicians and sociologists passing off their all-embracing theories as scientific. Metaphysic might be stimulating; it could never be prescriptive.

Scientific method implied being accessible to challenges devised by others. Hence knowledge could not be a matter of personal conviction, however sincere; nor could an untestable theory be warranted by the intuitive genius of no matter how brilliant a prophet or seer. For anything to qualify as knowledge it had to be open to examination, and to the risk of disproof, by the most rigorous possible critics. Fallibility was not evidence of the weakness of a theory; on the contrary, the possibility of refutation guaranteed engagement with reality. Theories that were alleged to be about the world, but which could never *conceivably* be falsified, were for that reason *not* about the world.

Marx and Freud, however seductive their critical or diagnostic astuteness, were revealed to be unscientific by their *systematic* inability to imagine, let alone supply, circumstances under which their ideas might be proved fallacious. If, through the elasticity of its terminology, a theory could always explain away whatever phenomena might seem to render it erroneous, it could not be scientific. Popper did not deny that Freud and Marx were *interesting* and innovatory as moralists or social critics; what he denied, fervently, was the claim, as dear to them as to their followers, that they were scientists.

The philosophers of the influential Vienna Circle – among them, Rudolf Carnap and Otto Neurath – seemed to concur with Popper. As 'logical positivists', they had argued that any proposition that could not be verified was meaningless. Positivism intended to banish metaphysics from intellectual esteem. It aimed to establish the universality of the scientific outlook. Only the propositions of natural science could be said meaningfully to be true. However, logical positivists faced a central problem, albeit an old one, concerning verification. David Hume had pointed out – embarrassingly for those who sought absolute certainty – that there was no logical reason to believe that, because the sun rose yesterday, and this morning, it would *certainly* do so tomorrow. Such arguments from induction, on which science was said conventionally to be based, could claim only that, after an indefinite number of regularities had been observed, it was irrational, although never strictly illogical, not to accept that what happened before would happen again. 'If p, then q' might express something incontrovertible in logic (depending, of course, on the values of p and q); but in the physical sciences it could never be *logically* certain that effect would follow cause. In view of this, the verification of a scientific law could never be conclusive. Popper maintained that unless the problem of induction could be resolved (and, he insisted, it could *never* be), positivism's Verification Principle had no warrant to ascribe meaning to science.

How true could scientific truth be, if it was based on nothing more secure than a series of observations and on the consequent assumption, at some indeterminate moment, that the Universe would henceforth honour its contract with science by maintaining an observed consistency? Popper proposed that the problem of scientific method, and hence of verification, be looked at in a different way. In fact, he insisted, it was not the case that scientific thought proceeded on the basis of accumulated observations of regularities. Scientific theories were *never* inductively proved by virtue of a plethora of instances that, at some moment, amounted to a law. Absolute verification was a chimera. Fortunately, however, there was no call to remain racked by the uncertainty that induction failed to dispel. In science, the hypothesis came *first*; tests and observations followed. No heap of observed instances either prompted a theory or amounted to a proof, as inductionists implied. What lent plausibility to scientific hypotheses – which, in practice, were often proposed on the basis of no preliminary observations whatever – was their ability to survive stringent challenges that their authors or their peers devised to test them.

Science did not proceed by showing why, or that, certain things happened; it established that – if a theory were valid – certain things could *not* happen. For instance, 'One cannot carry water in a sieve' is a theory that no sane man would seek to verify by filling a succession of sieves with water and seeking to carry them to a given point. We begin to recognize something to be the case when to deny it would be to fly in the face of demonstrable facts. By the same token, science cannot 'discover' a tautology, since to deny it is merely self-contradictory. All theories, such as Marxism, which affect to be infallible can only be elaborate tautologies, protected from refutation by their circularity. For simple instance, 'What will happen will happen' is irrefutable only because, although it may *seem* predictive, no possible event or non-event in the future can prove or disprove it.

Ancillary to Popper's vision of science was that of the scientist as an honest man. Civilization and science were intimately linked in the sociology of knowledge. The personal honesty of a researcher might be admirable, but it could never supply a validation. A scientist's work had, by definition, only to be open to honest scrutiny by his peers. Such openness to challenge was integral to progress. In science there might be guesswork; there could not be privilege. Scientific method was both central to human progress and a paradigm of responsible community. No scientist could claim to have struck theoretical gold without making his findings available to public assayers. And when the alchemist was found not to have turned lead into gold, he could not save his theory by redefining his lead as a

8

special form of gold. Genius might (as Einstein did) amaze, but it could not *by itself* certify: without the humility to endure examination, there could be no valid pride in achievement.

In pseudo-science as practised by Freud or Marx, ideology can make facts accord with anything if its terms are sufficiently elasticized (and elusive). The critics of such ideologies can be systematically dismissed by their proponents, since *in the terms of the system* they can always be accused of being, for instance, either 'in denial' or 'lackeys of the bourgeoisie'. In the same way, those who questioned the tenets or authority of the Catholic Church could be anathematized as heathens or heretics or apostates. In such totalizing world-systems, there *could* be no disinterested critic, since there was no room in their conception of the Universe for anyone to be free of their all-consuming, all-explaining logic. No Archimedes could find a platform from which to lever them from infallible omniscience.

Popper's *Logik der Forschung* (translated as *The Logic of Scientific Discovery*) unveiled his principle of fallibility. When it appeared in Vienna in 1934, it was more or less favourably reviewed by members of the Vienna Circle, to which, though never an adherent, he remained personally tangential. However, Popper's challenge to inductionism was held, by its author at least, to have killed off logical positivism. It is certainly the case that the notion of verifiability – over which A.J. Ayer was to muse, futilely as he admitted, for many years – never became a feasible measure, still less a logical determinant, of meaningfulness.

As a result of his book's success, Popper was invited to England during 1935 and 1936. If his anti-inductionism was not well received (and sometimes derided), he made literally vital contacts with the British philosophical establishment: he was soon to be offered academic posts that would enable him to remove himself from Austria. Although his parents had renounced Judaism, in which he never showed much interest, he would undoubtedly have been defined as a Jew by the Nazis. There may be no causal link between his rejection of what he was to term 'essentialism' and the racist notion that 'once a Jew always a Jew', but it would be implausible not to see some psychological connection between his personal circumstances and the urgency with which he denounced the specious logic of totalitarian doctrines.

By the time war broke out in 1939, he had already sketched out the arguments that were to appear as *The Poverty of Historicism*. However, the material was rejected by, among others, the English philosophical journal *Mind* and did not find a publisher until 1944. Popper was offered hospitality at Cambridge in 1936, but he had already applied for, and secured, a teaching post at the University of Canterbury, in New Zealand, where he and his wife, whom he had married in 1930, spent the war. While engaged in arduous teaching duties, and without the use of an adequate library, he wrote both *The Poverty of Historicism* – on which I propose to concentrate in this monograph – and *The Open Society and Its Enemies*, whose densely annotated two volumes are, to a considerable degree, amplified (and impressively ponderous) pendants to the first book.

Popper's notion of scientific method remained fundamental to the political thought that he called his war work. Although he was far from any battlefield, the peaceful seclusion of New Zealand did not calm his conscientious

10

horror at the murderous effects of what he was to call 'historicism'. *The Poverty of Historicism* carries a dedication 'In memory of the countless men, women and children of all creeds or nations or races who fell victim to the fascist and communist belief in the inexorable Laws of Historical Destiny'.

His critics often winced at the caustic rhetoric with which Popper pressed his case (he had become a master of the English language, though no habitual user of understatement). His lack of temperance meant that his war work, like Orwell's *Animal Farm*, did not find an eager publisher. When *The Poverty of Historicism* and, in particular, *The Open Society and Its Enemies* were finally printed, the author's exaggerations were often cited as an excuse for dismissing his case. His attacks on Aristotle were held to be improperly irreverent and those on Plato – more thoroughly argued, but also more virulent – were said by entrenched Platonists to be lacking in scholarship. Popper had taught himself Greek in order to read Greek authors (Heraclitus was also the subject of his scourging admiration), but he had been somewhat reliant on translations which, in the unendowed state of the libraries at Canterbury, were sometimes not as good as they might have been. Those who wish to examine the attacks made on his readings of Plato (and his replies) will find a useful compendium in *Plato, Popper and Politics* (1967), edited by Renford Bambrough.

The publication of *The Open Society and Its Enemies* owed much to the advocacy of Ernst Gombrich and Friedrich von Hayek, who had made good their transition from Vienna to English academic eminence. With their sponsorship, Popper was soon recruited to a readership at the London School of Economics, where he later became a professor. From

1946 onwards, his life was based in England. His assimilation was celebrated by a knighthood in 1967.

Popper's marriage was both childless and, reports indicate, not particularly happy. However, his intellectual partnership with his wife was sustained until her death in 1985. In the following year, he was a visiting professor in Vienna. He continued to engage actively, and often aggressively, in philosophy and in practical politics, almost to the end of his long life in 1994. He published prolifically, on a number of topics, but his fame rested on his notion of 'the open society', even though he considered his contributions to the philosophy of science, such as *Conjectures and Refutations* (1969) of at least equal importance.

Karl Popper was not, as they say, an easy man. He was both opinionated and touchy. If he advocated public discussion, he was quick to scorn those who doubted him. In the gossip of academics, it was said that *The Open Society* had been written by one of its enemies. On one famous occasion, at the Moral Sciences Club in Cambridge, he and his fellow ex-Austrian Wittgenstein almost came to blows. Bertrand Russell is said to have stepped between them, after which Wittgenstein slammed out of the room. Freud might have ironized on what he once called 'the Narcissism of small differences', though neither man would have been likely to acknowledge that there was little to choose between their views.

Popper's intolerance of others lends comedy to his championship of the sociology of knowledge and to his advocacy of a willingness to be criticized, but it does nothing to damage the logic of his case. One of the central aspects of Popper's position, on both science and politics, is his insistence on the importance of *institutions* in the conservation of freedom and of knowledge and in creating an arena for their interdependent propagation. It was never impossible that a fool should propose a valid solution to a problem, even if it was by chance; whoever we are, your theory and mine must both be tested in the hard, even light of public scrutiny. Neither your eminence nor my obscurity could *guarantee* the wisdom or entail the folly of our ideas. However inconveniently for tidy theorists, chance too played a part in social and scientific history. As the discovery of penicillin showed, scientists often stumble on a solution before they have posed the problem.

Popper's campaign against historicism was conducted on the same principles that he declared mandatory in the advance of science. He said that he had not, at the time of their discovery, considered their application to the social sciences, in which he had yet to become interested. He claimed that this lack of preconceived purpose rendered all the more striking the relevance of scientific methodology to areas where he had not previously considered applying it. Since his demand for refutability had not been devised specifically to demolish historicist theories, he could not be accused of premeditated partiality when it happened to destroy their pretensions. Since both Marxism and Social Darwinism (on which Hitlerism relied to justify its ruthlessness) claimed to be at once incontrovertible and scientific, what was intended to prove them invulnerable was revealed to be their failing.

In view of Popper's passionate opposition to totalitarianism, it must have given him some satisfaction to live to see the collapse of both Hitler's Germany and Stalin's USSR. Each had based barbarous policies on pseudo-scientific philosophies defective alike in logic and in humanity. Since

Popper regarded democracy as the only political system capable of institutionalizing knowledge *and* freedom, and since he regarded the latter as a condition for the former, it may be said – though he might not say it – that history had proved him right. The fallibility of the democracies had turned out to be a strength; the infallibility of dictators had revealed their weakness. Totalitarian systems created an illusion of frictionless cohesion and inflexible unanimity, but – by damning all dissent as treachery – such régimes lost any prospect of improvement or self-correction through constructive criticism.

THE POVERTY OF HISTORICISM

Popper was a philosophical polemicist whose battles, when he began to fight them, were of urgent significance. The success of his campaign has, perhaps, rendered his belligerence somewhat obsolete. Victory has left his enemies free to accuse him of a want of subtlety and an excess of animus. His importance, it is argued, was transitory and his time is past. There is facile optimism in this claim. The notion that we have nothing more to fear from ideology – implicit in Fukayama's Popperian book about 'the end of history' – has helped to bury Popper under garlands of obituary appreciation. However, it may be too soon to assume that uncontrolled liberalism is now and for ever the only viable (or plausible) system. It is also dubious whether Popper would have endorsed a world order in which economic might is always right.

When he challenged the inevitabilities of historicism, it

was because he was convinced that he knew the correct way for scientific inquiry to be conducted (and that no theory was correct unless scientific). Recently, there has been a reaction – for example, on the part of Lewis Wolpert and David Papineau – against the idea that we need, or can sustain, a philosophy of science along Popperian lines. Whether or not this challenge is justified, I cannot judge. Fortunately, nor need I: Popper's assault on historicism loses little of its persuasive force even if (as I do not believe) he was completely wrong about scientific method.

Popper's political writing may have been fortified by his philosophy of science, just as, in another context, Bertrand Russell's opinions on morals and society seemed (in some eyes) to be certified by largely unread works of genius such as *Principia Mathematica*. In logic, Russell's views on marriage or the hydrogen bomb were in no way sustained by his mathematical brilliance, although his and the public's confidence in them was probably strengthened by it. In the same way, Popper's faith in his ideas may well have derived from the precocious originality of his philosophy of science. Certainly that faith armed, and informed, his sociological studies. But even if his conception of scientific method were to merit refutation, his criticism of historicism would not on that account alone be nullified.

In the view of his admirers, he was often right about aspects of ideology. He had few rivals (Raymond Aron is the most formidable) among intellectuals when it came to opposing the tyranny not only of tyrants, but also of their intellectual apologists. The political theorists whom Popper thought most dangerous, and wicked, based their programmes on a cluster of pseudo-scientific or pseudo-logical notions about history, its course and its supposed laws.

The view that history had an inevitable direction and an immutable final destination, which was, so to say, written in the stars, and from which it could and should not be diverted, was common to both fascism and communism. Popper termed this common factor a belief in historicism, which he defined as

an approach to the social sciences which assumes that *historical prediction* is their principal aim, and which assumes that this aim is attainable by discovering the 'rhythms' or the 'patterns', the 'laws' or the 'trends' that underlie the evolution of history. [*PoH*, p. 3]

He refers with constant derision to both historicism and historicists, not hesitating to name names (Plato, Hegel and Marx in particular), but no less often ascribing to an unspecified historicist arguments that he then proceeds to dismantle. This method opens him to the charge of fabricating accessible targets. The usual philosophical retort to the attribution of untenable pronouncements to some generalized Aunt Sally is to exclaim 'But who ever said this?' Popper's prolonged disclosure of his sources in *The Open Society and Its Enemies* responds very thoroughly to this question. In the text, he declared his *parti pris* without hesitation, but he also took honest pains to make the best possible case for historicism, with certain elements of which (though never its conclusions) he confesses his sympathy. Would he have written with such obsessive vigour had he not recognized the formidable qualities, as well as the fundamental flaws, in the intelligences with whom he engaged? In view of his days as a communist, it would not be reckless to say that it was because he understood the temptations of historicism that he considered its refutation to be so important.

Although social Darwinism, with its affectations of conformity with the laws of nature, gave certain versions of fascism a spurious underpinning of scientific plausibility, the main thrust of Popper's reasoned indignation was against Marxism, which was a worthier (and hence more dangerous) enemy of the open society. The intellectual precedents for Marx's theories had a certain respectability, assuming that Hegel was respectable. As for Marx's moral indignation at capitalism's ruthless treatment of the working class, Popper shared it. He never took the view that, because change was not inevitable, nothing should or could be changed. On the contrary, his belief in indeterminism warranted, and demanded, what he called 'piecemeal social engineering'. He did not object to social (or even socialist) experiment, in controlled doses, where its effectiveness could be measured and tested, in a properly scientific way. His steady purpose was to question the effectiveness and, finally, even the *possibility* of long-term, Utopian planning, whether or not it was said to be consistent with the inevitable course of history.

Historicists claimed, and had to claim, that

> some of the characteristic methods of physics cannot be applied to the social sciences, owing to the profound differences between sociology and physics. Physical laws, or 'the laws of nature', ... are valid anywhere and always; for the physical world is ruled by a system of physical uniformities invariable throughout space and time. Sociological laws, however, or the laws of social life, differ in different places and periods ... [Historicism]

> denies that the regularities detectable in social life have the character of the immutable regularities of the physical world ... They depend on a particular *historical situation*. [Op. cit., p. 5]

Popper both presents the case candidly and admits some of its plausibility. He concedes that there are good reasons for *not* assimilating social laws (e.g. those of economics) to immutable laws of physics, on the grounds that historical periods can lead to radical changes in them. Is it not true that, unlike the laws of nature, social laws are man-made and hence can be changed by human decision? While pointing out that even the 'laws' of physics are subject to variation (water does not boil at 100 degrees centigrade regardless of the altitude at which the kettle is switched on), Popper accepts that reform, change and even revolution can be practical possibilities. His regular target is not the idea of change, but the idea that there can be a *law* of changes and, above all, that such so-called laws can certify long-term predictions.

Marxism, in particular, proclaims its oracular powers, against which there can be no appeal: once history has spoken, through the uniquely prescient voices of those who have cracked the code of its immutable changes, there is nothing more to be said or done, except to prepare the way of The Future or, in Marx's phrase, to 'ease its birth-pangs'. Historicism typically emphasizes the supposed futility of the experimental method in sociology, since experiments

> are not made to advance knowledge as such but to achieve political success. They are not performed in a laboratory detached from the outside world; rather, their very performance changes the conditions of society.

They can never be repeated under precisely similar conditions since the conditions were changed by their first performance. [Op. cit., p. 9]

Later, the historicist is credited with believing that

Even if the ordinary methods of physics were applicable to society, they would never be applicable to its most important features: *its division into periods, and the emergence of novelty.* Once we grasp the significance of social newness, we are forced to abandon the idea that the application of ordinary physical methods to the problems of sociology can aid us in understanding the problems of social development. [Op. cit., p. 11]

The claim that (modest) social measures are futile, since they are almost certainly devised merely to win votes, was first implied by Plato's indictment of Athenian democracy. Popper points out that unrepeatability in exactly similar laboratory conditions does not prove an experiment's futility (which *can*, however, be more or less strongly suggested by its *failure*); nor is exactitude always a condition of scientifically useful testing. He insists again and again that sociology can and should observe the rules of other sciences. What he does not seem to envisage is the argument that a one-party state *might* supply conditions under which limited social experiments could be undertaken by the government without the dreaded consequences of its eviction, should even well-intentioned measures fail to produce their hoped-for dividend. It seems that Popper does not give due weight to the possibility of avoiding the ochlocracy (mob rule) that Plato deplored, without going all the way with historicist deference to long-term inevitabilities. Can we not ask whether the one-party state *has* to be run on historicist principles? Popper's answer is implicit. He advocates that sociology should be systematically aware of what he calls 'the logic of the situation'. Since the one-party state must, by definition, imply that opposition is either forbidden or repressed, the experiments conducted by its rulers, however philosophical, can never be duly monitored or challenged. Freedom and division are, it seems, inseparable.

Popper's allegiance to democracy is unsentimental; if he regards it as the best way of avoiding bloodshed when governments fail or fall, his principal reason for favouring it is that its institutions are always likely to be uniquely congenial to the scientific advances on which mankind's future happiness (or lessening of unhappiness) depends. The kind of science that Popper valued had to have room for the unprogrammed discovery, for the maverick spirit, for the theorist who finds more than he is looking for.

It was Picasso who said, 'Je ne cherche pas, je trouve', but Popper's man of science was entitled to make the same claim. Once he had found what he was not looking for, however, he had to design public tests to validate his heuristic skills. The sort of state science that endorsed, for instance, experiments in eugenics, as the Nazis did, might be acceptable to men like George Bernard Shaw, whose tendency to admire dictators sprang from his own blithe delusions of superiority, but it was not an option for a surly humanist like Popper. Shavian eugenics – which involved euthanasia – were not accidentally anti-democratic: one of the first steps had to be to disenfranchise those whose unsuitability or uselessness made them eligible for superfluousness. There is a connection, in the logic of the situation, between open societies and the legal institutions that they alone spawn. For instance, a type of state-run medicine, where the Hippocratic code is rewritten by social Darwinism or Marxism, can sponsor murderers in white coats or the strait-jacketed travesties of Soviet psychiatric hospitals.

Historicism is said to be inclined to stress the importance of prediction as one of the tasks of science. Popper agrees, up to a point: however, he does *not* believe that *historical prophecy* is (or can be) one of the tasks of the social sciences. Historicism mystifies the subject by claiming that only the expert, or philosopher-king, has the intellectual capacity for prophecy. Popper offers an instance of the inherent difficulty of such predictions:

> Suppose … it were predicted [in some kind of oracular register] that the price of shares would rise for three days and then fall. Plainly, everyone connected with the market would sell on the third day, causing a fall of prices on that day and falsifying the prediction … *exact and detailed* scientific social predictions are therefore impossible. [Op. cit., pp. 13, 14]

The particular example is open to objection. The Marxist, for instance, might limit (or expand) his prediction to say only that the stock-market would – and should – be consigned to the dustbin of history. He might also say that Popper's example was both frivolous and irrelevant. Marxism was never intended to supply an inside track for fund managers. It claims that what matters, if we wish to understand and foresee its future development, is the history of the group, its traditions and institutions. Popper is not appeased:

Such considerations strongly suggest ... a close connection between historicism and the so-called *biological or organic theory* of social structures – the theory which interprets social groups by analogy with living organisms ... Similarly, the well-known theory of the existence of a *group-spirit*, as the carrier of the *group-traditions*, although not necessarily itself a part of the historicist argument, is closely related to the holistic view. [Op. cit., p. 19]

'Holism' in Popper's bestiary of aberrations, is not quite as bad as historicism, but it manifestly shares the totalitarian view that there can be no effective small-scale changes in society: what holism calls for, by definition, is wholesale planning. Only by replacing the entire machinery of an obsolete or immoral society (evolutionists like C. H. Waddington tended to conflate them) can durable reforms or revolutions be made. Holism is almost synonymous with Utopianism, which is the well-intentioned, certainly idealistic (*ergo*, in Marxist eyes, impractical) version of what Marxists have in mind when they tell us what the classless society will be like after the state has withered away.

Popper's attitude to group-spirits and the traditions that they carry may indicate his scorn for Jung, whose amalgam of psychoanalysis and fanciful, unprovable theories qualifies him as a pseudo-scientist. Jungian ideas belong, if at all, in a dubious category of the knowledge accumulated in what Popper chose to call 'World 3'. He gave this uncatchy title to the whole compendium of humanly fabricated and scientifically established knowledge. Its accumulation, over the millennia, has created what mankind calls objective reality. Popper accepts (and even insists) that subjective impressions can pass over into the category of objective knowledge, provided they coalesce into testable theories. In this way, he avoids, or postpones, the Kantian issue of a metaphysical reality outside man's intellectual or sensible grasp. If appearances are our reality, then they are, since we cannot transcend them. What we cannot properly do is what intuitionists and prophets affect to do, which is to 'know' what lies beyond the limits of human knowledge. There can, and will, be additions to World 3, thanks to science, but no one can trump it with superior certainties.

An unconvinced critic might say that World 3 was merely a more solid structure that serves in much the same office as Jung's group-traditions. Be that as it may, it is perhaps less the traditions than the groups to which Popper takes individualistic exception. He would insist, however, that the price of respectable entry into World 3 has to involve the same test of refutability that no holistic theory can ever pass.

HISTORICISM AND SOCIETY

The historicist is said to claim that 'physics aims at causal explanation: sociology at an understanding of purpose and meaning'. Hence he maintains that the latter has prompt, and proper, recourse to intuition and imagination, neither of which can be expected to propound theories that can then be tested. On the contrary, their rare quality is, allegedly, to offer a privileged method of untestable theorizing – for instance, about national character or the spirit of the age. Popper's response is to list three versions of intuitive understanding, in ascending order of delusiveness.

The first asserts that a social event is understood when analysed in terms of the forces that brought it about, i.e. when the individuals and groups involved, their purposes or interests, and the power they can dispose of, are known. The actions of individuals or groups are here understood as being in accordance with their aims – as promoting their real advantage or, at least, their imagined advantage. The method of sociology is here thought of as an imaginative reconstruction of either rational or irrational activities, directed towards certain ends.

The second variant goes further. It admits that such an analysis is necessary, particularly in regard to the understanding of individual actions or group activities. But ... more is needed for the understanding of social life ... [A] social event ... changes the situational value of a wide range of other events ... demanding a re-orientation and re-interpretation of all objects and of all actions in that particular field ... Thus in order to understand social life, we must go beyond the mere analysis of factual causes and effects ... [and] understand every event as playing a certain characteristic part within the whole. The event gains its significance from its influence upon the whole, and its significance is therefore in part determined by the whole.

The third variant ... goes even further ... It holds that to understand the meaning or significance of a social event, more is required than an analysis of its genesis, effects, and situational value ... it is necessary to analyse objective, underlying historical trends and tendencies ... prevailing at the period in question, and to analyse the contribution of the event in question to the historical process by which such trends become manifest. A full understanding of the Dreyfus Affair, for instance, demands over and above an analysis of its genesis, effects, and situational value, an insight into the fact that it was the manifestation of the contest between two historical tendencies in the development of the French Republic, democratic and autocratic, progressive and reactionary. [Op. cit., pp. 20–22]

It may well seem that there is a good deal of sense in these claims on behalf of intuitive understanding. Would Popper have spelt them out so elaborately if he had not recognized it? He did not think it wrong for historians to use wit and imagination in evaluating aspects of their subject. Where he became apprehensive was the point at which the fruits of imagination were wrapped in the language of science. They were then held to establish 'historical trends or tendencies [and] to a certain extent the application of *inference by analogy* from one historical period to another'. [Op. cit., p. 22]

This kind of reasoning was used, Popper recalls, in order to postulate a tendentious similarity between Greece before Alexander the Great and southern Germany before Bismarck, thus justifying as historically inevitable the latter's aggressive *Realpolitik*. Popper was eager to puncture grandiose theories with pointed ridicule. For instance, he piqued Hegel's logic of astronomy by pointing out that Hegel proved that a certain planet could not exist only shortly before its existence was established by observation. His derisive zeal disposed some philosophers to accuse Popper of vulgarity. It was, very often, the vulgarity of a man who had personal experience of the way in which murderous schemes could be derived from sublime and unchallengeable intuitions:

> the method of historical understanding does not only fit in with the ideas of holism. It also agrees very well with the historicist's emphasis on novelty; for novelty cannot be causally or rationally explained, but only intuitively grasped. [Op. cit., p. 23]

What is offensive is the intrusion, by apparently reasonable steps, of a notion of evidence that depends only on the authority of intuition. It leads to an absolute reliance on the power to persuade rather than on the ability to demonstrate in a challengeable way. The *Führerprinzip* is an example of what happens when rhetoric supplants reason. Art may supply beauty; it does not generate truth. Applause is not a form of proof.

It does not follow that it is wrong to have enthusiasms or, indeed, intuitions. There is nothing wrong, in principle, even in guesswork. But, if he wants them to be acted upon, the honest man, typified by the scientist, has to devise ways of establishing the validity of his intuitions *in public* and in accordance with the principle of refutability. Hence what is objectionable in the historicist is his flight from reason and from reason's dull accomplice, measurement. By alleging that there is no way of measuring the qualities of states, economic systems or forms of government in *quantitative* terms, the historicist claims that the laws of the social sciences, if there are any, must be *qualitative*. And qualities, whether physical or not, can be appraised only by intuition.

On this (false) account, it appears plausible to maintain that social science can never be scientific in Popper's sense. What alarms him, however, is not the allegation that social science is not exactly like physics. (Popper claims neither that it should nor that it could be, though he does think it has important similarities to natural sciences.) The scandal, for him, was that historicists and holists alike proceeded to claim that they were still scientists, but of a different, more far-seeing brand. For Popper there could be no such category of visionaries. Scientific methodology was one and indivisible. In this respect, it is interesting – and even amusing – to observe that Popper continued to share the typically Viennese urge to discover a universal morality, or logic. Having found it in science, he had no more tolerance for deviant ideas than the prophets, such as Marx and Freud, whom he denounced.

If it would be a mistake to charge Popper with sharing the ideologue's irrationality or pre-emptive self-righteousness, he was undoubtedly as fierce for reason as a reasonable man could well contrive. At the same time, he insisted that the use of reason was a human choice, not a natural characteristic. The point had been brought home to him when he accused a Nazi of lacking sound arguments. His opponent flashed his revolver and said, '*This* is my argument.'

It is indisputable that we are always free to use brutal or unreasonable methods, in the sense that no natural embargo prevents us, but we should not then be surprised to arrive at brutal or unreasonable conclusions. However, we should be *extremely* surprised, as Schopenhauer pointed out, to arrive by these means at reasonable ones. To be reasonable requires decision and application. Within reason itself, there are important decisions to make and a choice of methods to apply, good and bad. Getting things right depends on using valid terms and arguments. We may arrive first at a conclusion, but it cannot of itself be conclusive.

Popper's quarrel with Plato begins here. The greatness of Plato was never denied; his genius had issued in a formidably persuasive lobby for ideas that were at once superbly argued and fundamentally flawed. The source of much error was what Popper called essentialism, of which Aristotle too was a towering, if somewhat less purposeful, proponent.

The source of essentialism lay in Plato's Theory of Forms or Ideas. As Popper explains in vol. I of *The Open Society and Its Enemies* (pp. 27, 28):

> The Theory of Ideas demands that there should be only one Form or Idea of man; for it is one of the central doctrines of the Theory of Forms that there is only one Form of every 'race' or 'kind' of things ... similar things are copies or imprints of *one* Form ... In *The Republic* ... Plato explained his point ... using as his example the 'essential bed', i.e. the Form or Idea of a bed: 'God ... has made one essential bed, and only one; two or more he did not produce, and never will ... For ... even if God were to make two, and no more, then another would be brought to light, namely the Form exhibited by those two; this, and not those two, would then be the essential bed'.

What in this antique theory was, in Popper's view, so relevant to modern political theory that it required long, polemical attention? In the context of historicism, Plato's doctrine of a single true form of everything to be found on earth supplied a noble warrant – what A. J. Ayer would call an 'argument from piety' – for a misconceived reading of social realities. The influence of *The Republic*, seconded by a perverted version of Socrates' inquisitive method, had inspired social theorists to search for, and propose, the 'real' (immutable and, for some, God-given) meaning of such crucial terms as justice, society, freedom and life. The Platonic–'Socratic' line was to claim that, until we knew what 'justice' was meant, ideally, to be, we could not contrive its equivalent on earth. Only philosophers could be relied on, by virtue of their genius, to perceive and define the *essence* of these God-given meanings and so to ensure that human institutions conformed to the heavenly plan. Such a metaphysic claims that, unless our terminology is substantiated by what George Steiner terms 'real presences', words can have no valid meaning. No reliable conclusions can be drawn, it is claimed, from arguments unanchored in metaphysical reality.

Popper was not alone in arguing for the systematic delusiveness of first defining one's terms; he pointed out that biology – the science of life – has functioned perfectly well without having to define what 'life' means. The quest for the universal or real meaning of any word or term was not merely futile but misguided. The correct attitude to words was to be found in nominalism, which regards them as 'useful instruments of description' rather than as the encrypted carriers of God's true meaning, which had to be discovered by some guild of intuitional diviners.

Popper's assault on essentialism was purposeful as well as philosophical: 'it has ... been suggested that *while the methods of the natural sciences are fundamentally nominalistic, social science must adopt a methodological essentialism'* [PoH, p. 30]. This 'must', he maintained, is tendentious. After positing what affects to be a viable alternative to the methods of the natural sciences, the argument has insisted that the method alone is relevant to sociology. So? In the grim light of Marxism and its practice, Popper fears that the 'anti-naturalistic doctrines of Historicism' lead directly to the notion that it is possible, and important, to discover historical laws or trends. Such discoveries, although undiscoverable in Popper's view, will then be paraded as inevitably true. They will be accompanied by the assertion that it is, by definition, *morally* improper, no less than futile, to tamper with the inexorable (and inhuman) progress of history.

Having claimed that their style of political theorizing conforms to scientific principles, historicists insist on 'the importance of successful prediction and its "corroboration" '. Popper concedes that, up to this point, he has no large methodological quarrel with his opponents. What is intolerable to him is when they move on to say, for example, *'If it is possible for astronomy to predict eclipses, why should it not be possible for sociology to predict revolutions?'* [Op. cit., p. 36]

As soon as this demanding inquiry is made, it is often modified. After all, if such a possibility does exist, might it not – *should* it not? – be validated by a display of successful predictions? In order to avoid being put to specific tests, the historicist's answer is that 'qualitative' changes cannot be measured precisely. Instead of backing down, however, he takes convenient refuge in maintaining his ability to make long-term predictions or large-scale forecasts. The convenience lies in the fact that the truth or falsehood of long-term predictions lies 'over the horizon'. Vindication or disappointment is often beyond access in the lifetimes of those who are, more often than not, called upon to sacrifice themselves for the sake of another generation, which can, in its turn, be called upon for further necessary sacrifices.

Thus the coming of the classless society, like that of the Messiah, has to be taken on trust. The Marxist state of unalienated humanity lies on the unseen side of the foreseeable struggle, which must lead to the disappearance of capitalism. Because it is the nature of humanity, or at least of the bourgeoisie, to kick against the pricks, the withering away of the state and the end of alienation may be delayed, for instance, by the necessity to impose the 'dictatorship of the proletariat'. We can and must trust the evolutionary logic of history, but we have to accept that the future cannot, of its nature, be experimentally procured now.

Unfortunately for this kind of argument, Popper has a better one: the reason, he maintains, that we can *never* accurately predict the future – and this 'never' is logical, as well as practical – is that it is impossible for men to know now what they, or other men, *will* know in the future. Hence we are never possessed of the data that can allow us to make certain predictions about what may lie over the horizon of our present stock of knowledge. Marx, for instance, had no notion of modern industrial methods or energy-production, still less of the forms of economy that would be created *as the result of his own analysis of economic conditions and prospects*. Marx's predictions procured their own negation by alerting those who might have suffered from them of the measures they should take to counteract them. In this sense, he resembled the man who, by predicting that the stock market will fall at the end of the week, makes sure that, as a result of others acting on this information, it will fall *before* the end of the week.

Historicist historians are more impressive when they point out past inevitabilities than in divining them in the future. It requires no experiment to conclude that what has already happened could not not have happened. The past is not, however, a test-bed for the future. No historian's hindsight, however shrewd in its observations, cannot generate sufficient kudos to warrant putting our faith in his foresight. No intuition is required to discover that we cannot change (though we can certainly re-describe) what has already happened; this is true by virtue of a simple tautology. Unfortunately or not, no conclusions can be drawn about the predictability of the future from the fact that historians have uncovered the causes of what happened in the past. Historians, however objective they think themselves, are always selective. The choice of causes or reasons for any historical event is legion; even the event itself is an artificial construct. It is often arbitrarily defined and may well be compounded of many events (the French Revolution is an instance).

The difficulty about *why* things happen in history is that, unlike in a controlled scientific experiment, it is very difficult (not to say logically impossible) to isolate a historical event. It is even more difficult (and, as it were, *more* impossible) to determine definitively what is and is not relevant to its happening. Byron was alert to this when he remarked on the disproportionate effect of historical trifles such as the relations of Mrs Masham with her sovereign on the evolution of the Duke of Marlborough's career. Tolstoy, on the other hand, challenged the Great Man theory of history by discounting the significance of, in particular, Napoleon, but also of Kutuzow, the successfully obstinate Russian general, in turning the great tides of human change. Hegel was less decisive: when Napoleon rode in triumph through Jena, the philosopher regarded him as a 'world-historical' figure, but his veneration did not survive Bonaparte's eclipse.

Popper conceded a measure of merit to both points of view, without yielding an inch to systematic historicism, of which Tolstoy was clearly a somewhat casual adherent. When we get to programmatic systematizers, scientism leads us along a road paved with facile arguments of the following order:

> since [detailed forecasts] … are confined to brief periods … if we are at all interested in social predictions, large-scale forecasts (which are also long-term forecasts) remain … not only the most fascinating but actually the only forecasts worth attempting … [One] of the characteristic claims of historicism which is closely associated with its denial of the applicability of the experimental method, is that history, political and social, is the *only* empirical source of sociology … [Historicism] demands the recognition of the fundamental importance of historical forces, whether spiritual or material; for example, religious or ethical ideas, or economic interests. To analyse … this thicket of conflicting tendencies and forces and to penetrate to its roots, to the universal driving forces and laws of social change – this is the task of the social sciences, as seen by historicism. Only in this

way can we develop a theoretical science ... whose confirmation would mean the success of social theory ...

Sociology thus becomes, to the historicist, an attempt to solve the old problem of foretelling the future; not so much of the future of the individual as that of groups, and of the human race ... it could thereby become the foremost instrument of far-sighted practical politics. [Op. cit., pp. 38 et seqq.]

Popper proceeds, not a moment too soon, to make a distinction between prediction and prophecy. For him, the only honest predictions are technological. Predictions of this kind (assessing the tolerances of metal, the load-bearing limits of reinforced concrete, etc.) form the basis of engineering. It is typical of Popper's roots in continental tradition that he held the 'engineer' in high esteem, even though both Plato and Aristotle, not to mention Oxbridge dons of the old school, regarded such practical men as 'banausic'. For Popper, the engineer was a paragon of the practical man: he dealt with 'designed experiment, as opposed to mere patient observation' (or absurd specula-tion). It was not to be denied that impracticality yielded its fruits – for instance, in astronomy – but that was because they proved germane to practical predictions: for instance, when they were of meteorological value.

Popper proceeds with occasional, and significant, wari-ness, before resuming his polemical course:

I only wish to stress that historicists, quite consistently with their belief that sociological experiments are useless and impossible, argue for historical prophecy – ... of social, political and institutional developments – and against social engineering, as the practical aims of the social sciences ...

The kind of history with which historicists wish to identify sociology looks not only backwards to the past but also forwards to the future. It is the study of the operative forces and, above all, of the laws of social development ... not the pseudo-laws of apparent constancies or uniformities ... in order that men may adjust themselves to impending change by deducing prophecies from these laws. [Op. cit., pp. 44, 45]

The wariness derives, I suspect, from a certain nervousness in the introduction of the notion of 'the engineer' as a paradigm of the kind of practical man whose experience is not only useful, but also crucial to the running of a social machine. 'Piecemeal social engineering' will soon be advanced as the only proper way of tinkering with societies, purposefully but without exaggerated expectations or immodest blueprints.

In some respects, Popper never renounced a certain idea of socialism. His problem was to make an unbridgeable distinction between his kind of meliorism (involving making things better, or less bad) and the ideologist's aggressive optimism (involving helping to make things as good as they could possibly be, as God, or Marx, intended). That they shared certain common hopes did not, he insisted, entail that he was simply less energetic or less committed than his opponents. Differences of style *are* differences of content: because perfection is unattainable, to sacrifice blood in its pursuit is not only cruel but fatuous. Science can never have an end (Popper entitled his intellectual autobiography *Unended Quest*) and hence the question of

35

means is capital. While art, and perhaps Popper's beloved music in particular, need not – perhaps *must* not – care about means (the method of procuring sublime results), politics procures no exemption from humane procedures. Socially speaking, means are among, and perhaps indistinguishable from, our ends. Civilization is a matter of deciding to use reason both in the evaluation of our prospects and in the avoiding of wars, massacres and social degradation.

The historicist scorns such amiable caution. He insists that

> the real outcome will always be very different from the rational construction. It will always be the resultant of the momentary constellation of contesting forces. Furthermore, under no circumstances could the outcome of rational planning become a stable structure; for the balance of forces is bound to change. All social engineering, no matter how much it prides itself on its realism and on its scientific character, is doomed to remain a Utopian dream ...
>
> Historicism ... does not teach that nothing can be brought about; it only predicts that neither your dreams nor what your reason constructs will ever be brought about *according to plan*. Only such plans as fit in with the main current of history can be effective ... Social midwifery is the only perfectly reasonable activity open to us ... based on scientific foresight. [Op. cit., pp. 47, 49]

Historicism denies to human reason the power to bring about a more reasonable world. Marx famously observed that philosophy had so far only described the world and that what it now had to do was to *change* it. However, the deposit of his mature theories, so Popper insists, is that a historicist like Marx ends up by telling us that even he can only *interpret* social development and aid it in various ways, but that *nobody can change it*. Is there something a little glib in paying Marx back so neatly in his own coin? Popper asserts that he is merely criticizing attempts to link historicism with optimism or activism. If Marx and his like are right, there is in fact nothing necessarily good to be hoped for and, in addition, there is no way of helping to procure it. Activism, so far from being a logical adjunct of communist doctrine, is a fifth wheel on time's chariot, which (on Marx's analysis) has its own wings anyway.

Popper could not forget the essentialist argument advanced by German (and other) communists who, having defined fascism as a temporary, and *necessary*, stage on the road to communism, therefore did nothing to prevent Hitler's access to power on the grounds of 'the sooner it comes, the sooner it's gone'.

Wittgenstein once famously observed that 'philosophy leaves everything as it is'. Popper would have been justified in adding the rider that *bad philosophy* is liable to leave nothing as it is. Bloody consequences flow from embracing the wrong model for thought; neither sincerity nor good intentions can excuse the abuse of reason. We may all be entitled to our opinions, but it is decidedly not true that all opinions are of equal merit.

> – the consistent historicist will see ... a useful warning against the romantic and Utopian character of both optimism and pessimism in their usual forms, and of rationalism too. He will insist that a truly scientific historicism must be independent of such elements; that we simply have to submit to the existing laws of development, just as we have to submit to the law of gravity. The historicist ... may add that the most

37

reasonable attitude to adopt is *so to adjust one's system of values as to make it conform with the impending changes.* If this is done, one arrives at a form of optimism which can be justified, since any change will then necessarily be a change for the better, if judged by that system of values ...

The historicist's moral theory which could be described as 'moral futurism' has its counterpart in an aesthetic modernism ... [Op. cit., pp. 53, 54]

Comrade Pangloss is clearly in Popper's sights, but (not unusually) there is an interestingly suggestive aside, which is not followed up, about aesthetic inevitabilities. The glide from moral futurism to aesthetic (post-)modernism may owe its symmetry to a typically Viennese trope, curtly echoed by the young Wittgenstein in his *Tractatus-Logico-Philosophicus*, where he *equates* ethics and aesthetics. What deserves attention is the degree to which the cultural priority of modernism may have been foisted on us by notions of aesthetic inevitability that derive their force from the inevitability that is said, by Marxists, to belong to political development. The idea of a *single* correct aesthetic current is akin to that of a single correct political direction. Conceptualism is only the latest version of art that validates itself on the grounds of aesthetic premeditation. It is no accident, as Marxists used to say, that this puts artists under the ideological command of those – curators, journalists, dispensers of the residue from lotteries – who affect to predict which movement must be conducive to the Future of Art. Thus the avant-garde persists, albeit under new colours, when the rest of the Marxist army has been disbanded.

THE NATURE OF PROGRESS

If social change is not obligatory in the nature of things, on what grounds is it desirable and how is it to be contrived? Popper's answer to the second question is similar to the old one of how porcupines make love: very, very carefully. As to the first, need it be answered at all? If man is not perfectible, no more is he perfect, hence his situation can be improved. However, instead of wholesale plans to destroy whatever is not ideal and to begin again from scratch, Popper advocates 'piecemeal technology', made articulate by a process of critical analysis. Von Hayek had already said that 'economics developed mainly as the outcome of the investigation and refutation of successive Utopian proposals'. Such modesty seems wise, when it concerns prudent adjustments of already functioning institutions, but uneasiness sets in when Popper explores the argument that it is

> a technological problem ... of a public character [to discover whether] state management of production, is compatible with an effective democratic control of the administration; or ... *how to export democracy to the Middle East*. [Op. cit., p. 59]

The italics are mine, and I think I am entitled to them. It probably always was, and certainly is now, an extraordinary task to allot to a technological engineer to find a way to export *democracy* to the Middle East. Surely democracy and armaments cannot be packaged in quite the same kind of vessel. If the exporting of democracy was only an example, it remains a dubious one. How can it chime with Popper's belief, expressed elsewhere, that the social engineer has to take his cue, and his funds presumably, from political decision-makers, and that he himself does not implement specifically political ideas? How should we devise an unspecific export model of democracy that would be as purely structural as, say, the kit for an industrial plant? Could it be sold with confidence, or even honesty, to those unfamiliar with parliamentary processes and to the notion of majority rule and the compromises it involves? Ernest Gellner's studies offer evidence of the categorically undemocratic principles of Muslim societies. Can one legitimately, or honourably, insist that democracy is always ideologically neutral?

The primacy of the West (the home of science) is implicit in Popper's philosophy, just as it was in Marx's. I suspect that he took for granted a decline in the political significance of religion in the post-war world. He never discusses religion as anything but a personal choice of morality, to which harmless notions of salvation might attach. If he can, at times, accuse his Christian opponents of being unchristian, he means little more than that they are failing to love their neighbours. It suggests a want of practical imagination to insist that democracy can be 'sold' to Muslim societies, which are, rightly or wrongly (but who is to say?), disposed to regard it less as a panacea than as a Trojan horse containing alien and divisive forces. In this case at least, the proposed means by which change is to be procured cannot fall convincingly under the bland rubric of piecemeal technology.

There is another objection. Popper would not have us ask the essentialist question, 'What does democracy (really) mean, entail, involve?', but that will not prevent the question being posed, and with some urgency, if democracy is to be part of an export drive. Whether or not we choose to define it exactly, there *has* to be some consensus about what is meant by democracy. The Stalinist coinage 'People's Democracy', like the Nazi term 'People's Court', is laughable where it is not nauseating, precisely because we know that the terms 'Democracy' and 'Court' were being used in a perverted way: that is, not in accord with what we call their real meaning. Our knowledge of this is lodged, so to speak, in Popper's 'World 3'. That we cleave to these meanings as immutable is why arbitrary despots, from Robespierre to Pol Pot, excite outrage when they deform them.

On this account, the distinction between essentialism (bad) and nominalism (good) looks to be somewhat less abrupt than Popper claims. It may be the case that we do not need to define 'cricket' before we knock a ball about, but we do discover, and quite soon, that there have to be rules, and that what is against the rules is 'not cricket'. Purely verbal definitions, however strict, will never (and should never) be the means of imposing conclusions on mankind that are neither humane nor – whatever the pretence – necessary. However, rules do determine how a game is to proceed: elastic as they may be (or may be found to be), they do define – supply limits to – what constitutes playing the game, or not. We may not be able to say, ahead of time, what precise breach will dispose us to say 'it's not cricket any more', but it remains true that cricket cannot change into football and still be called cricket.

Nominalism taken beyond its (essential?) limits becomes indistinguishable, in its evasive self-validation, from the alchemy of those who can arrange never to be wrong. To talk of games and rules is not, in this context, light-hearted. Wittgenstein's question 'Can you play chess without the queen?' addressed the same topic. If the tone was playful, the issue is not. There was a kind of ghastly facetiousness in the use of the vocabulary of morals and responsibility by both Nazis and Soviet rulers, who knew very well that they were cheating. In a century of vicious parody, a sense of humour can be overused. If we mean to export democracy, we had best be clear what we mean by it.

Popper might have protested that he was advocating nothing more peremptory than the development of institutions and practices that might wean the Middle East from unsociable confrontations on the basis of previously irresoluble differences. He cannot, however, be acquitted of a programmatic complacency when it comes to the application of 'piecemeal social engineering' when the project is both large and without precedent. He observes, a little later, that

> piecemeal social engineering resembles physical engineering in regarding the *ends* as beyond the province of technology ... In this it differs from historicism, which regards the ends of human activities as dependent on historical forces and so within its province. [Op. cit., p. 64]

Respectability seems to derive from avoiding affectations of certainty in the results of an undertaking. But it is to strain an analogy to equate 'exporting democracy' with building a bridge or widening a road. Friedrich von Hayek had advanced an argument against centralized planning (and thus against large-scale social engineering) which impressed Popper. It was that 'the typical engineering job involved the centralization of all relevant knowledge in a single head, whereas it is typical of all truly social problems that knowledge has to be used which cannot be so centralized' (Hayek, *Collectivist Economic Planning*, 1935, p. 210). Popper draws the inference that 'the engineer must use the technological knowledge embodied in these hypotheses which inform him of the limitations of his own initiative as well as of his knowledge'. [Op. cit., p.64 note]

It could be argued that these limitations have been considerably broadened by the accumulation of knowledge in computers of whose power and accessibility Popper was no more prescient than Marx was of the advanced industrial methods that would make nonsense of his theory of surplus value. Does the single head model not lose some of its force when the planner can, with the aid of a computer, have two or three heads, as it were, at his fingertips? It may be said that such knowledge, drawn from elsewhere, might not be of the right kind; it might derive from unreliable, ideologically distorted sources. But Popper would not deny that scientists had a wider view when carried on giants' shoulders. Why should this not be true of planners?

Popper would probably not be fazed by this objection. For him the difference between piecemeal and Utopian engineering was that between the possible and the impossible:

> one is possible, while the other simply does not exist …
> while the piecemeal engineer can attack his problem
> with an open mind as to the scope of reform, the holist

cannot do this; for he has decided beforehand that a complete reconstruction is possible and necessary. [Op. cit., p. 69]

Unless one defines a complete reconstruction as meaning only that *nothing* that was there before can be allowed to survive, need the distinction be as logically abrupt as Popper would have it? Haussmann's radically re-planned Paris is still, manifestly, Paris. Popper would probably find this instance irrelevant. His target is typified by the Utopianist Karl Mannheim, when he says 'the political problem ... is to *organize human impulses* in such a way that they will direct their energy to the right strategic points and steer the whole process of development in the right direction'. This kind of project, Popper tells us, clearly discounts any possibility of testing the success or failure of the new society: 'Wholes in the [sense] holistic can never be the object of scientific inquiry' [Op. cit., p. 74]. That is reason enough for the holistic approach to merit anathema.

When Mannheim says that we must set up and direct the whole system of nature, he is telling us, so Popper insists, that we are *forced* to a logical impossibility. Hence he cannot be right. It remains an open question whether 'exporting democracy' would be any less of an attempt to 'steer the whole process of development in the right direction'.

WHAT CAN AND WHAT CANNOT BE DONE?

Popper insists, again and again, that 'not one example of a scientific description of a whole, concrete social situation is ever cited'. In today's (temporarily?) unideological climate, where non-democratic blocs do not seriously challenge western complacency, one is free to wonder whether Popper's adherence to the notion that science alone can provide a comprehensive model for human progress (towards an end we will never see and need not define) is not itself, however genially, ideological. He seeks, like any reasonable man, to discountenance false gods, but he never engages seriously with the notion of divinity. As a result, he seems hardly to notice the deep social and intellectual divisions implicit in the variety of religious response to the human condition. If we dismiss religion as dated mystification, we risk seriously misreading mankind. Whether or not we can prove, rationally, that God exists (clearly we cannot), we are still faced with Pascal's neat observation that the heart has its reasons. Neither the physical shape of the world nor the forms of human thought would be as they are, or have begun to be as they are, without the dimension of the sacred, without the fear of gods and the habit of obedience to divine ordinance. Human credulity may be a folly; religion may have done more harm than good (if such a balance sheet is conceivable); yet to strip out the spiritual and replace it only with science might be – to reverse the parable – to drive out seven demons and replace them with one. As one modern philosopher puts it, 'the remorseless secularism of those Austrians – that was what made Wittgenstein (who was one of them) come out fighting!'

Popper's own view, manifest in his sympathetic scolding of John Stuart Mill's 'psychologism', was that, since we cannot legislate for the vagaries of human nature, we do better to build social institutions in which man's diversity can be housed and honoured than to seek to rebuild man himself. Popper's notion of political rectitude was that modest social ambitions, accessible to piecemeal achievement, were better than grandiose and uncontrollable master-plans. Was there in this an element of nostalgia for the Hapsburg empire of his youth, in which, under a happily incompetent central authority, all kinds of ethnic communities agreed to differ? Austro-Hungary was written out of history by the master-plan of Versailles, an instance of grandiosely inept planning to which Popper barely refers, except to ironize about self-determination.

Popper retains a measure of faith in piecemeal experiments. He gives as an instance 'an experiment in socialism carried out in a factory or village'. Except in the case of modest 'pilot-schemes', it is hard to imagine what such an experiment could prove, or disprove. The Israeli kibbutz, for instance, was a brave experiment (although tainted, in some eyes, with Platonism), but it has, in the long run, proved only how difficult it is to sustain a cloistered social system in a larger society that has rejected its brand of Utopianism. The kibbutz movement was intended to be a model of co-operative living, and still has its proud adherents, but even its successes did nothing to justify, or prompt, imitation on a national scale (which might have involved something like the coercive nightmare of Soviet collective farming). On the simplest level of communication theory, it is impossible to argue from the viability of small communities (where votes and policies can be determined in almost daily conclave) to the virtue of organizing nation-states on similar lines. The ancient city-state *could not* expand and remain democratic, on the Athenian model, for that reason, among others. When the *demos* spoke, in Athens, they could literally be heard; when modern democratic politicians affect to listen to the people's voice, it is a rhetorical courtesy. Small ideas, when watered, cannot be relied on to grow into fertile big ideas. The dinosaur dies; the lizard lives.

Popper's determination to find only negligible differences between the methods of the natural sciences and those of the social sciences offered a trenchant method of criticizing ideology. It supplied no very convincing means of replacing it. The irony is manifest: Popper admired Marx for the sharpness of his criticisms of capitalism, but found him deficient when it came to proposing practical measures for its replacement. He might reply that it is not regrettable to lack a large scheme for organizing mankind. However, it is naive, or disingenuous, to presume that science and democracy are neutral and unaggressive ideas, which, in genial tandem, will avoid the horrors visited on humanity by unproven and unprovable certitudes such as Marxism.

Popper wants politicians to be more like scientists:

> Scientific method in politics means that the great art of convincing ourselves that we have not made any mistakes, of ignoring them, of hiding them, and of blaming others for them, is replaced by the greater art of accepting the responsibility for them ... and of applying

this knowledge so that we may avoid them in the future.

[Op. cit., p. 88]

But was it not almost exactly with this argument, and for the same reasons, that Plato proposed the replacement of democratic crowd-pleasers, grubbing for votes, with philosopher-kings whose immunity to election would allow them to transcend vulgar expedients and so create an Ideal State? Lenin's autocracy rolled along similar lines. The incapacity of actual tyrants (such as Plato's Syracusan protégé, Dionysius II) to measure up to expectations has never deterred advocates of the closed society from arguing the theoretical benefits of communities dominated by better or more enlightened tyrants or philosopher-kings. If Plato's ideas are to be rejected for their impracticality, why should we embrace the idea of a scientific democracy, which appears little more feasible, except on the grounds that it may be morally more amiable?

Popper's answer might be that democratic institutions can and often do, in fact, enable society to detect errors. By voting them out of power, it has bloodless means of sanctioning those responsible for mistakes. When businessmen make bad decisions, their balance sheets turn red; when they make catastrophic ones, their companies may be liquidated. This is painful for them, but endurable (even perhaps salutary, marketeers will argue) for the economy at large. But when centrally planned economies go grievously wrong, the entire society is traumatized. The failures of governments and companies in democratic societies suggest that the policies they have followed have been, in some metaphorical sense at least, refuted. Thus we may not be so far from a 'scientific' community as pessimists believe.

48

Popper claims that modesty of scale is part of any sound scientific method:

> it must be nearly impossible for us to persist in a critical attitude towards those of our actions which involve the lives of many men. To put it differently, it is very hard to learn from very big mistakes. [Op. cit., p. 88]

If we have had enough of macro-ideologies, the world remains in need of an *attitude*, if not of a scheme, for the betterment of mankind. Popper argues that

> a *systematic fight* against *definite wrongs*, against *concrete forms of injustice or exploitation, and avoidable suffering such as poverty or unemployment*, is a very different thing from the attempt to realize a distant ideal blueprint of society. [Op. cit., p. 91]

The italics are again mine. They emphasize the temptation to pass off measures of which Popper approves as 'piecemeal', and hence feasible, while maintaining that communists, holists and Utopianists are alike in baying for the moon. The notion that the terms emphasized are either easy of definition ('wrongs', for instance) or susceptible of piecemeal treatment deserves, but does not get, the rigorous self-scrutiny of which Popper was such an advocate. If piecemeal engineering ever had or ever could be the instrument of a 'systematic fight', there would be no need whatever for the holistic, Utopian schemes (or systematic fights) against which Popper so righteously, and rightly, protested when the wrong people were to be in charge.

Where Popper proves most convincing is in refusing to accept the theoretical distinction between (refutable) scientific claims and the historicist's claim to have knowledge –

by infallible intuition – of the laws of historical change. Such a distinction, if it were not false, would discriminate in favour of historicists. But it is false.

> In the natural sciences ... we can never be quite certain whether our laws are really universally valid ... [but] we do not add in our formulation of natural laws a condition saying that they are asserted only for the period for which they have been observed to hold ...
>
> If we were to admit laws that are themselves subject to change, change could never be explained by laws. *It would be the admission that change is simply miraculous. And it would be the end of scientific progress: for if unexpected observations were made, there would be no need to revise our theories: the ad hoc hypothesis that the laws have changed would 'explain' everything.*
>
> *These arguments hold for the social sciences no less than for the natural sciences.* [Op. cit., pp. 102, 103]

Again the italics are mine. They emphasize a point on which Popper is unflinching and, it seems to me, unarguably correct. There can, he concedes, be a historicist hypothesis which holds that the task of the social sciences is to 'lay bare the *law of evolution of society* in order to foretell its future ... the so-called "natural laws of succession", if only because there can be a *hypothesis* of almost any kind'. The historicist claim is said to be a concoction of astronomy, Darwin and millennarian religious and metaphysical beliefs.

> This [evolutionary] hypothesis is not a universal law ... It has, rather, the character of a particular (singular or specific) historical statement ... the fact that all laws of

nature are hypotheses must not distract our attention from the fact that not all hypotheses are laws.

But can there be a *law* of evolution ... in the sense intended by T. H. Huxley when he wrote: '... he must be a half-hearted philosopher who ... doubts that science will sooner or later ... become possessed of the law of evolution of organic forms – of the unvarying order of that great chain of causes and effects of which all organic forms, ancient and modern, are the links ...'[?] I believe that the answer to this question must be 'No', and that the search for the law of the 'unvarying order' in evolution cannot possibly fall within the scope of scientific method, whether in biology or in sociology ... Such a process ... proceeds in accordance with all kinds of causal laws, for example, the laws of mechanics, of chemistry, of heredity and segregation, of natural selection, etc. Its description, however, is not a law, but only a singular historical statement ... [Op. cit., pp. 106, 107, 108]

We have ... no valid reason to expect of any apparent repetition of a historical development that it will *continue* to run parallel to its prototype. Admittedly, once we believe in a law of repetitive life-cycles [cf. Vico, Spengler, Toynbee, etc.] – a belief ... perhaps inherited from Plato – we are sure to discover historical confirmation of it nearly everywhere. But this is merely one of the many instances of metaphysical theories seemingly confirmed by facts – facts which, if examined more closely, turn out to be selected in the light of the very theories they are supposed to test ...

Of nearly every theory it may be said that it agrees with many facts: this is one of the reasons why a theory

51

can be said to be corroborated only if we are unable to find refuting facts, rather than if we are able to find supporting facts. [Op. cit., p. 111 and note]

Here Popper is at his most characteristic and persuasive. He also reveals very clearly why the logical positivists of his youth found him congenial: his attitude to 'metaphysics' is here as dismissive as theirs. (It is not inconsistent with finding 'some' merit in metaphysics as a speculative preliminary to scientific validation or literary insight.) What matters here is the inflexible rule that 'trends are not laws'. The logic of the 'laws of history' is not a scientific logic, but it seeks to draw credibility through the scientistic pretence that it is.

Although we may assume that any actual succession of phenomena proceeds according to the laws of nature, it is important to realize that practically *no sequence of, say, three or more causally connected concrete events proceeds according to any single law of nature* ... The idea that any concrete sequence or succession of events (apart from such examples as the movement of a pendulum or a solar system) can be described or explained by any one law, or by any one definite set of laws, is simply mistaken. There are neither laws of succession, nor laws of evolution ...

That [John Stuart] Mill should seriously discuss the question whether 'the phenomena of human society' revolve 'in an orbit' or whether they move, progressively, in a 'trajectory' is in keeping with this fundamental confusion between laws and trends, as well as with the holistic idea that society can 'move' as a whole – say, like a planet. [Op. cit., pp. 117, 118, 119]

Popper pays steady tribute to Mill, as he does to Auguste Comte, the founder of positivism, for their contributions to the methodology of science. What he challenges, implacably, is a kind of enthusiasm that extends the kudos of science to various kinds of crystal-ball gazing and seems to warrant its visions. It is no accident that the result, almost inevitably, is either a kind of callous resignation, in the face of unstoppable history, or a doctrine of heartless collaboration with the inhumanity of forces that we are powerless to control or avoid.

> This ... is the central mistake of historicism ... *its 'laws of development' turn out to be absolute trends*; trends which, like laws, do not depend on initial conditions, and which carry us irresistibly in a certain direction into the future. They are the basis of unconditional *prophecies*, as opposed to conditional scientific *predictions* ...
>
> ... we have all the time to try to imagine conditions under which the trend in question would disappear. But this is just what the historicist cannot do ... The poverty of historicism ... is a poverty of imagination. The historicist continuously upbraids those who cannot imagine a change in their little worlds; yet it seems that the historicist is himself deficient in imagination, for he cannot imagine a change in the conditions of change. [Op. cit., pp. 128, 129, 130]
>
> ... if we are uncritical we shall always find what we want: we shall look for, and find, confirmations, and we shall look away from, and not see, whatever might be dangerous to our pet theories. In this way it is only too easy to obtain what appears to be overwhelming evidence in favour of a theory which, if approached

critically, would have been refuted. In order to make the method of selection by elimination work, and to ensure that only the fittest theories survive, their struggle for life must be made severe for them. [Op. cit., p. 134]

Popper's furious hostility to bogus 'scientific' arguments on grand lines does not leave him blind to a certain need for sociological attention to larger issues. There is, he suggests,

room for a more detailed analysis of the *logic of situations* ... We need studies based on methodological individualism ... of the way in which new traditions may be created ... our individualistic and institutionalist models of such collective entities as nations, or governments, or markets, will have to be supplemented by models of political situations as well as of social movements such as scientific and industrial progress ... [Op. cit., p. 149]

It is possible, for example, to interpret 'history' as the history of class struggle ... or as the history of the struggle between the 'open' and the 'closed' society, or as the history of scientific and industrial progress. All of these are more or less interesting points of view, and *as such* perfectly unobjectionable. But historicists do not present them as such; they do not see that there is necessarily a plurality of interpretations which are fundamentally on the same level of both, suggestiveness and arbitrariness (even though some of them may be distinguished by their *fertility* ...). Instead, [historicists] present them as doctrines or theories ... And if they actually find that their point of view is fertile, and that many facts can be ordered and interpreted in its light, then they mistake this for a confirmation, or even for a proof, of their doctrine.

On the other hand, ... classical historians ... [aiming] at objectivity ... feel bound to avoid any selective point of view; but since this is impossible, they usually adopt points of view without being aware of them. This must defeat their efforts to be objective, for one cannot possibly be critical of one's own point of view, and conscious of its limitations, without being aware of it.

The way out of this dilemma, of course, is to be clear about the necessity of adopting a point of view; to state this point of view plainly, and always to remain conscious that it is one among many, and that even if it should amount to a theory, it may not be testable. [Op. cit., pp. 151, 152]

Somewhere behind Popper's allegiance to science (and thus to reason) there lurks an acknowledgement that it is *possible* that certain theories, even of ultimate destinations for man, might *turn out to be true* eventually. We may even all finally be hailed before God's judgement seat. But it remains unjustifiable, not to say immoral, to impose unproved truths – and their social consequences – in terms of class or exclusion, on humanity now, on the grounds that they may be proved valid in some inaccessible future. Since what will be known then cannot logically be known *now*, those who affect to pierce the veils of time and report what the future must hold are charlatans today, *even if they turn out to have been clairvoyants, come some distant tomorrow.* No doubt, there are those who would say that Chartres Cathedral, for instance, was a consequence of a scientifically unprovable doctrine. Indeed, myth has been, in many cultures, the unquestionable foundation of both art and literature. This objection has its force, which can be turned away, at least partially, by saying that theories of divine or metaphysical truth, of the kind that sponsored religious art and architecture, cannot be protected artificially against scientific criteria that were inapplicable when they came into being. Popper always conceded that the primacy of reason in human affairs was a matter of decision, not of natural necessity. Hence we must choose (if we can) whether or not we want to be ruled by creeds and credulities whose advocates have usually relied more on coercion than on choice.

Popper's scepticism is both methodological and humane. He is an indeterminist who is determined to accept no argument that our fate is not only fixed (which in some trivial sense it is, since what will be will be), but also predictable. Progress, he insists, is no more inevitable than decline and fall, even if we take all available steps to assist science in improving life:

> we cannot exclude the logical possibility, say, of a bacterium or virus that spreads a wish for Nirvana ... ultimately, much depends on sheer luck ... For truth is *not manifest*, and it is a mistake to believe – as did Comte and Mill – that once the 'obstacles' (the allusion is to the Church) are removed, truth will be visible to all who genuinely want to see it.
>
> ... the human factor is *the* ultimately uncertain and wayward element in social life and in all social institutions. Indeed this is the element which ultimately *cannot* be completely controlled by institutions (as Spinoza first saw); for every attempt at controlling it completely must

lead to tyranny; which means, to the omnipotence of the human factor – the whims of a few men, or even of one. [Op. cit., p. 157, 158]

But is it not possible to control the human factor by *science* – the opposite of whim? No, because that will interfere with the diversity of individuals ...

> Even the emotionally satisfying appeal for a *common purpose*, however excellent, is an appeal to abandon all rival moral opinions and the cross-criticisms and arguments to which they give rise. It is an appeal to abandon rational thought.
> ... The mainspring of evolution and progress is the variety of the material which may become subject to selection. As far as human evolution is concerned it [viz. the mainspring] is the 'freedom to be odd and unlike one's neighbour' ... 'to disagree with the majority, and go one's own way'. Holistic control, which must lead to the equalization not of human rights but of human minds, would mean the end of progress. [Op. cit., p. 159]

Progress is not a certainty, but a prospect. Reason is not part of human nature, but a choice which, alone, can encourage (and *construct*) tolerance and the rule of law. As the Nazi demonstrated, man can always draw his gun and put an end to arguments, or (if the weapon is large enough) to mankind. Nothing guarantees us a happy future or a wise choice, even where we choose freely and rationally. Individuality is necessary for diversity, as are well-manned institutions for the storage and testing of the theories that individuals propose. We can neither escape the unevenness of chance nor be sure how the unloaded dice will roll. Popper sees the good news and the bad news as almost indistinguishable; man can only do so much and yet there is no set limit to what he may do. He argues for foresight against prophecy and for small steps on reliable grounds rather than for a hectic faith in pie in the sky.

It could, however, be said that Popper's datedness is made manifest by the fact that he seems to rely on the machinery of democracy now in place, in civilized society, for further improvements in the human condition. What well-manned institutions, other than the governments of nation-states, are going to be able to inaugurate schemes of piecemeal engineering grand enough to deal with global pollution, genocidal oppression of minorities and pandemics such as AIDS?

The assumption that prevailing structures could deal with curable difficulties such as poverty and unemployment was naive even in Popper's day. How can global corporations, with their overriding influence, now be controlled by nation-state legislatures (or supernational congeries of ministers responsible to national electorates)? In a state of affairs where multinational conglomerates can afford to be indifferent to local laws and enrol corrupt governments to their service, existing institutions – whether or not they call themselves democratic – seem inadequate. Global corporations render piecemeal measures effective only against companies and individuals who lack the stamina and clout for economic survival. How, if at all, are major corporations, with transnational funds and managements, to be controlled by democratic authorities whose writs run only to their frontiers? A host of organizational questions of this sort confronts mankind in the coming millennium.

Popper's answer might be that we have no better choice than to arm ourselves with reason, to avoid fatalism and to try to make things less bad. If his advertisements for tolerance and patient effort were sometimes mocked by his personal style, it never disgraced them. Where he was right, he was magisterial; where he was wrong, he was – as in theory he might have wished – fallible.

Further Reading

Popper, Karl, *The Poverty of Historicism* (Routledge (ARK edn.), London, 1986, reprinted 1994).

Popper, Karl, *The Open Society and its Enemies* (Routledge and Sons, London, 1945. Golden Jubilee Edition, Routledge, 1995).

Popper, Karl, *The Logic of Scientific Discovery* (Hutchinson and Co., London, 1959, revised 1980).

Popper, Karl, *Conjectures and Refutations* (Routledge-Kegan Paul, London, 1963).

Popper, Karl, *Objective Knowledge* (OUP, 1972).

Popper, Karl, *Unended Quest* (Fontana, London, 1976, revised Flamingo, London, 1986. Routledge, 1992).

Bambrough, Renford ed., *Plato, Popper and Politics* (Heffer, Cambridge, 1967).

Corvi, Roberta, *An Introduction to the Thought of Karl Popper* (Routledge, London, 1997).

Magee, Bryan, *Popper* (Fontana, London, 1977).

Miller, David ed., *A Pocket Popper* (Fontana, London, 1983).

Shearmur, Jeremy, *The Political Thought of Karl Popper* (Routledge, London, 1996).